T0198944

From Lessons to Blessings

A Tribute to the Heroes in My Life

LEOLA M JONES

authorHOUSE®

AuthorHouse™
1663 Liberty Drive
Bloomington, IN 47403
www.authorhouse.com
Phone: 1 (800) 839-8640

Published by AuthorHouse 10/18/2018

ISBN: 978-1-5462-6321-0 (sc)
ISBN: 978-1-5462-6319-7 (hc)
ISBN: 978-1-5462-6320-3 (e)

Library of Congress Control Number: 2018911864

My Mother, Louise Turner

By Leola M. Jones

My Grandfather, Willie Turner)

By Leola M. Jones

"FROM LESSONS TO BLESSINGS"

A TRIBUTE TO THE HEROES IN MY LIFE

MY MOTHER, LOUISE TURNER
AND
MY MATERNAL GRANDFATHER,
WILLIE TURNER

Contents

Introduction

FROM LESSONS TO BLESSINGS

I have always thought that my life was ordinary. As I grew up, I realized that my life was not ordinary because of the lessons that I learned over the years. These lessons have made me who I am today. I have told them to others I have met along life's way.

When you are young, your world is your family, church members, neighbors, friends and school mates. My mother and grandfather were my heroes. To me, a hero is someone you respect or recognize for doing something that put you in awe of just knowing this person.

I loved my mother and grandfather. The two grown-ups that I listened to; tried to imitate; and I respected them for their life style, spiritual strength, and abundant love and affection shown to me and others.

I have always preferred to laugh rather than cry; to see the glass half-full rather than half-empty; and to belief that all things work out the best way even when I do not get the desired result that I want. Maybe next time I will get it right! Or, maybe it is just not for me! Then, I thank God that I recognized the fact that I am not the head of my life. God is!!! He knows what is best for me!!

I have collected essays and short writings since high school days. I have collected these writing for many years and they have brought me such awareness of Life. My individual responsibility in this world is to God, family and friends and in general all people.

I have always been thankful that I love people. I have been a talker since I was very young and love to play and tease others. My sister always used to say that if I stood next to a pole, I would talk to the pole. When you talk to people, you find out that most people are just like you. Some think that they are different but once you begin to talk, you realize that you have so much in common. LIFE!!!

I learned most of these lessons from my mother, Louise Turner, and my maternal grandfather, Willie Turner. They influenced me more than any other individuals in my life and the love I feel for my mother and grandfather has inspired me throughout my life. I have always felt loved and I have always had love in my heart for others. I am thankful that God placed so many wonderful people in my life. I count my blessings every day to have such beautiful people in my life!!!

These "Lessons of Life" that I have tried to remember and to live my life accordingly, are very important to me. I want to share them with you!!!

CHAPTER 1

My Mother, Louise Turner

When I think about all the roles we hold throughout our lifetimes, I marvel at how unique we are. My mother was a daughter, sister, mother, aunt, cousin, grandmother, great grandmother, employee, friend, neighbor, among others. The one that left such a great impression in my life was my mother, Louise Turner.

I grew up in Pine Bluff, Arkansas. We had good neighbors! Those days were different from the neighborhoods today. You knew your neighbor, and everyone looked out for one another. I remember that we used skeleton keys to lock our doors. If you lost your key, you just borrowed a key from one of the neighbors' since they were all the same skeleton key. We had a few elderly neighbors who kept up with everything that happened on the block. They watched us grow up over the years and gave their unsolicited comments on our actions, whether good or bad. We were taught to respect them, with no exception. If they saw us do something bad or heard us say something we should not say, it was like our mothers heard it and we would be punished. I would always speak to the neighbors. Sometimes, I would sit on their porches and talk with them. They used to laugh because they knew I talked too much but would not say that to me. The two sisters, Ms. Ida and Ms. Nettie, lived on the corner across the street; Mrs. Virginia lived to the right of them; and the most wonderful, generous and loving couple, Mr. & Mrs. Shackleford, lived on the corner. Ms. Elvira lived next door to me on the right side. Next door on my left were the Sanders, who had a child my age who I was very close to. The other neighbors on the block did not have any children. They watched us grow up and gave advice. We politely thanked them because we knew if we said or did anything disrespectful, Mama would not like that.

My mother was the second oldest daughter. My grandfather and grandmother used to call her "Sister". I don't know why, but I do know it was a loving term because I saw it in my grandfather's eyes and how he treated my Mother. This was Love and Respect between parent and child that I recognized.

My mother had one brother, Uncle Floyd, and three sisters, Lena, Dora and Katie (who died as a young girl before I was born). I saw how loving and protective Mother was about her sisters and brother. This was love and respect among siblings.

I don't remember too much until I was about three or four years old. My grandmother was ill, and I remember riding in the ambulance with my mother to take my grandmother to the hospital in Little Rock. My mother was very caring and attentive to my grandmother. This was love, respect and commitment to caring for her mother.

During my grandmother's illness, there was an ambulance driver I came to know. He would drive the ambulance to Little Rock for my grandmother's doctor visit at the hospital. My mother left me with the driver. We would sit and drink soda pop and wait. He would let me talk and I talked the whole time we were waiting. When the doctor visit was over, he would take us back home. I remember him being such a nice man, but I do not remember his name. Once he saw me playing down the street, he stopped his ambulance just to speak and hug me. This was love and respect of one of God's servants.

When my grandmother died, I remember that I was sitting on my mother's lap at the funeral and fell on the floor when she cried for the loss of her mother. I hurt when I saw that Mama was hurting, and I began to cry also. This love and respect, shown by my Mama for her mother, ignited a fire in me for my mother.

Mama Loved Her Children

I always liked being my mother's BABY. I thought that Mama was partial to me, but I later learned that she loved each of her children and respected each one's individuality. Our happiness and well-being were Mother's number one priority.

I remember that my older brother's friend came over to the house one day and my mother was wearing shorts. The boys told my brother that my mother was pretty and looked good in those shorts. Now, my brother was upset at the boys for looking at his mother and was slightly embarrassed. So, he asked Mama not to wear shorts. She said OK. She was true to her word. I never saw her wear shorts after that.

Mama Loved to Play

Mama loved to have fun with us. We raised chickens. To kill the chickens, Papa would just wring the chicken's head. Mama would tie a string on the chicken's neck and on the chicken's feet. Someone would hold the neck string, and someone would hold the feet string. Then Mama would chop the head off the chicken and the chicken's body would jerk on the ground. Mama knew that we were afraid of killing the chicken. One day she said something about how the chicken would not die and she started running after us. We ran from her screaming and she ran behind us. Our neighbors laughed because they knew Mama was playing with us.

On another occasion, the next-door neighbor thought that my brother broke his window. The neighbor started chasing my brother down the street. Mama ran behind the neighbor yelling "Don't hit my son!" The neighbor's wife ran behind Mama yelling "Don't you touch that boy." Again, the neighbors were laughing, and we were too.

Hit by a Car

I was hit by a car at Townsend Park. I was crossing the road in the park. I stopped, and the car stopped. I started, and the car started. The third time I started to cross, I just knew the car would stop. Well, the driver probably thought that since I stopped twice, I would stop the third time. The car hit me and knocked me across the road.

I was told not to move. An ambulance was called. People were trying to get in touch with my mother. She was at work. I think a couple of people called her. One told her one thing, and another told her another thing, and finally someone told her I had been seriously injured. The ambulance driver was told where my mother worked so he could pick her up on the way to the hospital. When the ambulance got there, my mother was climbing out the window. She told me that one person said I was hurt bad and another person said he thought I was unconscious. She was so nervous by the time we got there that she could not find the door to get out, so she opened the window and climbed out.

It was so funny watching my mother climb out the window. I started to laugh. When she looked for me and saw me laughing, she also started to laugh. She was so relieved to see that I was not seriously hurt. Years later, when I think about her love for me, I laugh at her humor and realize how blessed I am to have so much love.

You Can't Whip the BABY!!!

I loved the fact that I was the BABY! I am the youngest of my mother's children. I think that I was just a little bit spoiled. My mother had four children: my oldest brother, my sister, my younger brother, and then me.

I loved being the baby of the family. I usually was good because I liked to get compliments rather than any negative attention. I never liked being on punishment.

One day I did something I should not have done. My mother asked me, and I admitted that I had did it. She then said that I was going to get spanked (a whipping which I never liked even though I can count the punishments I received when I was young.) When my mother said that she was going to whip me, I looked at her and said," You can't whip me." "What did you say?" she asked. I repeated, "You can't whip me. I am the BABY!" Her answer to me was, "I will show you."

She gave me a few licks and I was crying so loudly, almost screaming, that everyone on the block heard me. Now, I must note here that she was using a cloth belt that did not really hurt me physically. What hurt me was the fact that I did not think that she should whip the BABY!

My mother explained that I did something that was wrong; and most important was that I did something I knew was wrong but did it anyway. She said that when you do something wrong, you must pay the consequences. If she allowed me to do wrong and did not punish me, someone would sooner or later; and that someone, more than likely, would hurt me much more than she would. She said, "You must take responsibility for what you do. For every bad action, there is a consequence that you will not like." Since I knew it was wrong and did it anyway, I had to pay the consequence of that bad action. Well, since I told her that I would not do it again, maybe she should have waited to see what my consequence was. That way I would not have two bad reactions to my one action. She said, "That is exactly what I am going to do - give you the reaction to your bad action now."

I cried and told my mother I loved her and would not do wrong again because I still did not like whippings. I was a good child, but imperfect. I did typical things children do but I never wanted to do anything that would embarrass my mother. Looking back, my mother was very smart. Most of us will think, when we remember the silly/dumb things we did, that we really were not very smart. Our parents knew us better that we knew ourselves. Later in life, I would observe my children and realize they were thinking of asking or doing something that may be a silly/dumb thing. I recognized the "thinking look" that my mother was aware when she studied my face.

Once my cousin tried to talk me into going somewhere without permission. She said we could have fun for hours and the whipping only lasted for a few minutes. Usually, me and another cousin would do things together. Mainly, because we were the same age, liked some of the same things, and we were a little slower and naïve than the others. Now, my aunt did not whip my cousins with a cloth belt like my mother. It was not the pain of the whipping but the realization that I was disappointing my mother.

I tried to remember that lesson when it came to making decisions whether I should or should not do something. Her punishment was easily forgotten but the idea of displeasing my mother stayed with me all my life.

The Wave

My Mother had a way of waving goodbye to me as I became a teenager. She would wave her hand left and right instead of up and down.

She said, "It is alright for your skirt to move left and right but do not move it up and down. There are so many wonderful things in your childhood that you must experience and enjoy before growing up. Don't grow up too fast!!!"

She said that I would think that I was in love many times before I would really find true love. In one year, I would not even remember his name or what I liked about him, but I would remember what I disliked about him.

She would always say that life if full of beautiful and ugly people, good and bad memories, good and bad choices, but once you make the decision to grow up too fast, you cannot take it back. Enjoy your youth, grow according to your personality (some grow up slowly and some grow up fast). Don't rush your life!!! I never told my friends why Mama waved left to right. It was my constant reminder whenever I left home.

Dream!!! Most young girls dream of college, getting married and having children. I always wanted to be a teacher and have two children. I never became a teacher. I married before I finished college. I am so happy that I never gave up my dream of a college degree, so I went back to college many times until I finished. I received an Associate Degree, a Bachelor of Science Degree and a Paralegal Certificate. Whenever I encountered difficulties in my working, school and family life, I remembered what my mother said. Her wave said take pride in yourself as a young lady; do not allow anyone to take advantage of you. Trust your heart! You will see the "real" person if you 'really' look/observe that person. Learn to never jump into hasty situations. I understand what my mother meant by waiting to grow up. I have always been a "child at heart" and enjoy the simple pleasures of life. I will find something to laugh about daily. I can always laugh at myself!!! I will not be offended!

I moved to Chicago to live with my sister. I got a job at the phone company; met an old friend and got married. When I became pregnant with my first child, I called Mama and asked her to come to Chicago. Now, remember that I always was very close to my mother and did not want to have a baby without her being with me. Mama left her secure environment and moved to Chicago.

I am Thankful for the Wave!!![1]

---

[1] A merry heart doeth good like a medicine: but a broken spirit drieth the bones. Proverbs 17:22 KJV

CHAPTER 2

My Grandfather, Willie Turner

My maternal grandfather (Papa as everyone called him) was very special to me. He was always there for me. He truly loved me, and I truly love Papa!!!

We (my mother, sister, and two brothers) moved in Papa's house before I was born. Later when my grandmother got sick, my mother helped with her. When my grandmother died, we stayed on.

Papa was over 6 feet tall. He broke his leg at work and walked with a limp. To me, he seemed very, very tall! He had a very strong, heavy, husky masculine voice. He always had a pipe in his mouth whether the pipe had tobacco or not.

I was the youngest of my sister and brothers. I was the "Baby" and his "pet." He was old fashioned and unchangeable until

I came along. As children, we could not play cards, dance, or play music. He referred to playing music as sounding like a "juke joint" or "barrel house" and would not allow us to play anything but church music, and that had to be played at a very low volume.

He always had a soft spot for me, probably because I was the only one that hung around him, hugging and kissing him, and singing and talking. I was an excessive talker who told everything. I would get on his knee and sing my childish songs to him, and he would tell me a story.

Papa's Truck

Papa had an old blue pickup truck. It had many dents and rusty spots. His usual speed never exceeded 15 or 20 mph like "a fast crawl."

One rainy day when I was in the 9th grade (I think), Papa came to school to pick me up. I saw his truck. The children teased me about how slow he drove. I did not want the kids to see me ride home in that "slow truck" so I slipped out the side door. He came home much later. He never said a word. He had waited in front of the school about 15 minutes before bell to about 15 minutes after bell. He never came to pick me up after that. I had hurt my grandfather. I felt ashamed of my grandfather's slow truck. How could I hurt such a wonderful man?

Days passed, and no rain was in the forecast. Papa continued to be loving toward me. I tried to be nicer to him. One morning I went into Papa's room before I left for school. I said "Papa, it looks like rain today. If it rains today, will you come pick me up?" He looked up and said, "Baby, do you want me to pick you up?" I said, "Sure Papa. You don't want your baby to get wet, do you?" He smiled, the biggest smile, "No, I don't ever want my baby to get wet." I kissed him and happily went to school.

That day it rained. His truck was first in line. I ran happily to his truck, got in and kissed him, and off we went home.

I felt so good!!! I never wanted to hurt my grandfather ever again!!!

Papa loved me so much he did not want me to get wet when it rained. His priority was protecting me. I did not know what priority I had? But, I learned never take a person for granted. The reward for loving another person is reciprocated love and respect. I know I had a great grandfather who loved me dearly. When someone loves you dearly and is willing to protect you and take care of you, that person should receive your love and respect as his is given to you. I truly loved Papa!!! Now, I knew that I truly respected Papa!!! I still feel his love today!!!

The Golden Rule

Papa used to say that there is one rule I must learn and always practice: "Do unto others as you wish them to do unto you." (Matthew 7:12 KJV) He said that if you keep your heart filled with love, you will not have room for hate. But, if you decide there is someone that you want to hate, think about your choice. Don't choose to hate! Choose to love!! Your hatred for that person does not affect that person's life but it will leave a negative effect on your life. When someone does wrong toward you, that is that person's sin. However, when someone does wrong to you and you reciprocate by doing something wrong to that person, you have sinned also. That takes me back to Papa's "devil take it" saying.

Devil Take It

Papa worked at a lumber company. He broke his leg which left him with a limp. If you remember the TV show "The Real McCoy's" staring Walter Brennan. He had a limp and when he walked fast the limp was even more pronounced. That was how Papa walked. If he was angry or in a hurry to go somewhere, he walked very fast.

When Papa got angry about something, he would stump around the house saying "Devil take it. Devil take it." I asked him why he kept saying "Devil take it. Devil take it." He told me that negative, angry emotions are choices that we make. He chose to give them to the devil. So, whenever these negative thoughts come into his mind, he told the devil to take them because he did not to want them.

One day, I got angry about something. I stumped around the house saying, "Devil take it. Devil take it." Papa saw me and said, "That's right Baby. Don't keep it. Give it back to the devil and you will feel much better." After that, I used "devil take it" as my cooling words to get any animosity out of my mind before it attacked my heart.

Growing Up

Papa had a kind heart. When it was lightning and thundering, I was afraid to be in the house by myself. If my mother was not at home, I would go get into Papa's bed. Well, as I got older, my mother told me I was too old to get in Papa's bed. But the next time it was thundering and lighting, I was afraid, so I got in Papa's bed. When she came home she said, "I thought I told you not to get in Papa's bed." I said, "You did, but I was scared." So, she told Papa that I was too big to get in his bed. The next time it was storming, I ran straight to Papa's bed and got in his bed. When he saw me, he just got up from his bed and sat in the chair. He never told me to go back to my bed. He knew I was scared. I was asleep when Mama got home and woke me up. Papa was still in the chair. Papa told Mama to leave me along. If I am afraid of the storm, he would help me to get over the fear of storms. Papa told me stories and laughed with me. He reassured me that he was only a few steps away. He said, "Now, when you grow up and have children, you will have to help your children get over fears of storms, monsters under the bed and the boogey man." When I had my daughter, she loved scary movies and I still did not like them. But I did get over storms.

Learning to Think of Others

During the summer when school was out, I was home with Papa. He would cook for me. We had a little joke. He knew I really liked to eat. I don't remember missing a meal. He would cook early just in case I got hungry. He would say, "I am full. Eat what you want and give the rest to the Red." Red was our dog! The joke was I always ate the leftovers. He used to cook ox tails, rice and cornbread fried in a cast iron skillet. He would shake the skillet then flip the bread in the air and catch it in the skillet every time. I ate everything Papa cooked except the hominy grits. I realized that he liked hominy grits but stopped cooking them because I didn't like hominy grits. I decided to ask for some hominy grits. He cooked what I liked to please me. So, I decided that if he eats what I like to please me, I should eat the hominy grits to please him. I asked Papa to cook me some hominy grits. To my surprise, I began to like hominy grits!

Papa Got A We Got

I was continually talking about something. I had very little quiet time. I would even talk to myself and answer me. One day, I heard my big brother and cousin sing a song. They were singing, "Papa got a we got. Papa got a we got." That was easy to learn so I went to Papa and told him I know a new song. Proudly, I asked if he would like to hear it. "Yes." He said. I began singing loudly, "Papa got a we got. Papa got a we got. Papa got a we got." I was so proud to learn the song because I thought it was a song that would please him since they were singing about Papa. Papa softly said, "Do not sing that song. It is not a song for good little girls to sing." Since I always wanted to be "a good little girl" I just said, "Okay." I never thought to sing that song again. I never realized until I was grown what the song meant. The boys had what papa had!

Over the Years

I moved to Chicago, married and had children, I always called Papa and checked on him. He could be funny without meaning to be funny. I can't remember how Papa got to Chicago to visit us. I do remember he was going to take the Greyhound Bus back to Arkansas. So, my daughter was about 7 or 8 years old. She has always been very observant. Once I took a package over to a friend's house. I put the package on the table. We visited for an hour or two. When we stood to go home, my daughter looked at me and then she looked at the package. She then walked to the table and picked up the package and walked over to me and took my hand to leave. I told her the package was for my friend. She took it back to the table and returned to take my hand to leave. After that, if I was taking something to someone, I mentioned it to her because I knew she was very observant of what I did.

I knew she would watch Papa like a hawk; and I knew that Papa was going to watch over her. They had a bonding trip.

Whenever I went back to visit Papa, I would always sit on Papa's lap and hug and kiss him. My children would do the same! They knew I loved Papa and he loved me. I knew Papa loved my children and they loved him. Showing love and affection is like a 2-way mirror. You get out of live what you put into it!!!

To me, my grandfather was a great man!!! He loved his family! He loved God! Whenever I think of Papa, all I feel is thankfulness for him being in my life!

I have always felt special because I know I AM LOVED!!! God loves me! Mama and Papa loves me! My family and friends love me! I meet strangers that love me. Why I know that, because I meet strangers that I love!! [2]

---

[2] A good man leaveth an inheritance to his children's children: and the wealth of the sinner is laid up for the just. Proverbs 13:22 KJV

CHAPTER 3

Goodbye to My Father

I was raised by my mother. My father came into my life after I finished high school. I learned a lot about my father from his cousin. His cousin still lived close and I used to visit them often. They were always happy to see me and so I relished them as I had no other relatives on my father's side of the family. I am sure that he was informed about what was happening in my life. I would stop by their house and talk to them often. Their house was between my Aunt Lena's house and my house, so I traveled that way regularly.

My father was a preacher. I grew up in the church he founded. The people there loved and respected him which made me very proud of him.

I moved to Chicago and got a job at the telephone company. During that time, you could make long distance calls to your family and friends. I called him very often and enjoyed talking with him. Through our many conversations, our relationship grew. He got to know me, and I got to know him.

My visits to see him were very pleasant and I enjoyed meeting all my sisters and brothers. I even had a sister with the same birthday I had. Over the years, some of my brothers and my sister have visited or lived with me.

I think that I did not want to love my father because I thought I was betraying my mother. I loved my mother very much and was prepared to tell him not to say anything negative about my mother. My mother never said anything negative about my father, which made me love and respect her even more. Well, he never said anything negative about my mother and that warmed my heart.

Over the years, I would often call and talk with him. He would call me if I went too long and did not call him. He would say, "Just calling to see how you are doing". I always ended the conversation with "I love you." The last conversation I had with my father I ended the call with the usual, "I love you." He said, he loved me. Then I said, "No, I really love you!" He laughed and said, "I always knew you did."

That was the last conversation I had with my father. Whenever I think of him, I think of our last words. It is a wonderful feeling to remember your last conversation with someone you love. I am so thankful to God!!! I was able to tell him that I truly loved him!! This realization cleared my mind and left me open to remember him with love and admiration in my heart. I have always felt uneasy with any negative emotions I felt. Sometimes, we think something that is not true. I realized that. Accepting love and giving love is the most beautiful feeling. [3]

---

[3] And now abide faith, hope, love, these three; but the greatest of these *is* love. 1 Corinthian 13:13 NKJV

CHAPTER 4

My Children, Michele and Mitchell

$\mathcal{I}$ have two children, Michele and Mitchell, whom I love very dearly. They are my pride and joy. I love them unconditionally. I have told them that I love them so very much and that will never change. I have not liked some of the things they have done, but my love for them will never change. I love to call them and tell them just how much I love them. I tease them; I "Baby Talk" them; I laugh with them; and I make sure that they both know how much I value my relationship with them.

After I retired, I moved back to Texas to be closer to them. I loved my life in Illinois and knew that I would really miss my wonderful sister and friends. However, I wanted to be closer to my children. I talked to them quite often, but I was so excited that I would be living in the same town and could see them. Just being closer to them has made me very happy.

My Daughter

Michele is my first child, "My Baby Girl". She has always been a strong individual since birth. She walked when she was about 9 months old. She never crawled!! She has always been very observant with a creative imagination.

She has always liked to dress up. She likes compliments. When her father worked nights, Michele would stay up until he came home. She would lay in the bed and as soon as he peeped his head in the bedroom, she would lift her arms for him to pick her up. She would fall to sleep watching TV with him. She was a "daddy's girl."

She has a creative mind. She was taking classes for journalism and I read one of her stories and it brought tears to my eyes. I hoped she would continue. Maybe after she reads this, she may want to show me the best way to write a book.

Once Michele's teacher told me that Michele disrupted his classroom. I asked what did she do? He said that he never saw her do anything. Everyone would be laughing except Michele. She would sit at her desk and show no emotions. He never caught her, but he knew it was her. That really sounded like Michele because she could say something funny and never crack a smile.

I think that when she was a young girl, I told her all the things that Mama told me. When Mama lived with us, Michele and Mama had a special connection. Michele and Mama would look at something then look at each other and laugh. I never understood their laughter, but then I never got the punch line on a joke. Michele would give Mama pedicures, manicures and wash and style her hair. Sometimes Mama would ask Michele to get her some water and Michele would not answer her. She would call her name again. Still no answer or acknowledgement from Michele. Then Mama would call her a little name and Michele and Mama would laugh and Michele would get up and give her a glass of water. They did not need words to communicate with each other. There was a special bond between them.

Mama had an aneurysm and could not walk. She regained her memory and I was thankful for her living with us because she gave my children plenty of advice. After she died, I found out that they told her a lot of things that they did not discuss with me. I was happy to hear that because everyone needs someone they can talk to without worrying if it will be passed along to others involved. She never told me anything. I believe that Mama would not ever reveal anything UNLESS it was something that she knew was above their comprehension and ability to resolve.

Mama had a great sense of humor. When we lived in Channelview, there was a small family cemetery behind our house. Mama told Michele and Mitchell that she saw a bug-like creature flying around with a human head, laughing, and looking for them. She described his small body, big head, and his big bulging eyes. It was hard to scare my daughter, but it was easy to scare me.

I have always been very proud of my daughter. She is strong yet compassionate, loving, kind, confident, with good qualities. I know she loves me. She knows I love her. I think that we have a great relationship and value it very much. I love my Baby Girl!!!

My Son

Mitchell is my second born. He is my "Baby Boy". Mitchell was born with a ventricular septal heart defect. Septal defects are sometimes called a 'hole' in the heart. At that time, it was the most common heart problem that babies were born with. This was corrected when he was 8 weeks old. He also had a valve and a half in one chamber and only a half in the other chamber. When he was 2 years old, he had open heart surgery.

Even though that was a scary part of my life, I have always been so thankful to be there with him during his surgery and recovery. His father had nicknamed him "Tiger." The staff put "Tiger" on his bed post and started to call him "Tiger". This really described how courageous he was. The first words the doctor spoke to me, after his 10-hour surgery, was "Thank God". It was different than what they initially thought, but the surgery was a success. The doctor looked at me after the surgery and told me I could go see him in recovery; gave me a number to call to check on him; and then told me to go home and take a sleeping pill. Each time I woke up, I would call the hospital. He was doing fine!

When I returned to the hospital the next day, he was still in intensive care. When he was put back into his room, I slept on a cot next to his bed. He woke up and cried "Mama, Mama." I would raise my head, so he could see that I was still there. I rubbed his hand and he went back to sleep. During the night, he woke up several times. He would move his hand and I would rub his hand to let him know that I was still there. As a parent, I have never been so thankful to God for watching over him, for the best spirit-filled doctors operating on him, and my wonderful son. He was only 19 months old, but with so much courage to deal with pain without fear. He would push the IV pole and walk a few steps, push the pole and walk until he got where he wanted to be. He did not cry from the pain. He just slowly walked. I had to tell him to rest. He missed his sister so much that I asked for permission for her to visit him. He stayed in the hospital for a month and I only left to check on my daughter. When I was not there, Mama would be there with him. He had a temperature and the doctors did not know why. Finally, he was going home, with the temperature. After he got home, the temperature finally left. He would climb on the couch and jump off and my heart would literally stop watching him. He never slowed down!!!

Five years after his surgery, we moved to Houston. He had developed a speech impediment – stuttering, if he got excited. When he was attending a school in Spring Branch he was "the Candy Man" in a play. He was so wonderful!!! As parents, we always think our children are great – but those who saw the play thought he did a great performance and started calling him "The Candy Man."

Michele and Mitchell later joined little league baseball teams. They played for two years. He was a fast runner and became a good batter. Adults place too much importance on their children winning. The most important factor should be the children playing baseball and the comradery and team-work gained from playing with others. My son should have won "the most improved player" on his team, but the coach gave it to his son. I asked my son what he thought about what the coach did. He said he felt sorry for the son of the coach because he lost out on a giving his son a wonderful growing experience. His son was embarrassed because he knew he did not earn the award. I was so proud of my son. Sometimes when people are not treated right, people get angry and elect never to do it again. He worried about the coach's son. He did not need the award. He just really enjoyed playing!

I could tell when my son was thinking of something to ask me. One day we were in a store and he said to me, "Mama, I will let you be good to me. You can buy me something." A lady behind me thought that was so cute. I knew he thought it out and said it for attention. I told him that I would not buy him anything. The lady thought he was so cute and wanted to buy it for him anyway. I told the lady that I am always good to him, BUT he will not get anything today. The show off!!!

My mother would eat pizza but did not really like pizza. My son liked pizza. But, if he was hunger, she would tell him to order them some pizza. He would sit in her room and talk with her. He decided that he wanted to help people. He was interested in nursing, when he was 12 years old. That would change many times. But his caring heart never changed. He always wanted to be helpful to people in need of assistance.

Mama's last visit to the hospital, I could barely understand what she was saying. I took my son into intensive care to see her. When she saw him, she said, "Mitchell, you are a good person. The Lord will bless you if you be yourself. Don't change who you are. Be yourself and you will be blessed." After I took him out and returned in a few minutes, she was not talking. I think she had said what she wanted to say. She really loved him. At her funeral, he asked me if I would get angry if he told me something. I said I would not get angry. He said, "I think I love Grandma more than I love you." That was the best compliment he could give me. I knew that what he really meant was that he really loved Mama. I said, "I am so happy that you love Mama that much because I love her that much too. I am so thankful that you showed her that much love."

I was so thankful that she lived those 10 years with us. The children had an opportunity to show love and compassion, to enjoy her sense of humor, to bond with her, and to learn humility. She blessed all our lives!!! She never talked about her condition. I was so blessed that she was home with my children when I was not able to be home. I was so blessed that my daughter and son really loved my mother!!! Mama really loved my daughter and son!!! I am so proud of the bond they shared with my mother! Mama would just look at you sometimes with a smile on her face. That smile was LOVE![4]

---

[4] A good [man] leaveth an inheritance to his children's children: and the wealth of the sinner [is] laid up for the just. Proverbs 13:22 KJV

CHAPTER 5

My Sister, Barbie

$\mathscr{I}$ think I have the best sister in the world!!! My sister has supported me all my life. We are very close, yet we would debate small differences, words and phrases, i.e., six or half-a-dozen.

Tattle Tale

When I was young, my sister had to babysit me when my mother was at work. Wherever she went, she had to take me with her. She used to tell me that she would dress me like her when I was out with her.

She would bribe me to not tell our mother where we went or who we talked to. I took the bribe. But, I would still tell Mama. I couldn't wait for Mama to come home!! We were walking down the street when I saw my mother on the porch. I started running down the middle of the street, shouting "Mama, Mama, guess what!!! I ran to her to tell my adventures of the day. Mama never asked me what we did so I had to volunteer. I remember one day we went to a club. It was closed and only a young boy, my sister, my cousin and myself was there. I played on the piano. I drank a soda pop. Plus, they gave me some money. I had a wonderful time!!

The problem was, I was so excited about having such a wonderful time that I couldn't keep it to myself. I just had to tell Mama!!!

My sister did not like me telling on her. She vowed that one day she would get me back for telling everything I told on her. She had to keep me when Mama went to work, so she had to take me with her. I did not pay much attention to her threats of getting me back. I usually kept the good thoughts and threw away the bad ones.

Look in the Mirror

I thought that my sister was pretty, and I always wanted to look like her. As a matter of fact, I thought that I was the "ugly duckling" in the family. I was the youngest child; the darkest; and I had hair that you had to wet to comb. I was the shortest. I was not as smart as my sister or brother. My sister was salutatorian at her school. My younger brother did not go to school one semester and went back to school and made good grades. I worked extra hard to get my grades.

Mama and my sister told me that I was beautiful. Mama said, "Your physical body changes over time as you age so physical beauty is not very important. It is not your physical looks that matters. What matters is who you are! You are what's in your heart, what you believe and how you live your life. Keep your heart and mind open to good things!!! Guard your heart and mind!!! You have no control over health issues, hard times, aging and other things you will face in this life."

My sister and mother dressed me until I was about 12 years old. They told me how pretty I looked. I looked in the mirror and did not see what they saw. But, I said, "If they said it, it must be true." SO, I saw the image in the mirror, but I looked not at the physical view but the love and trust I felt for them.

I always loved people. I always wanted to love people. I always knew that some people may not love me back, and that was alright because I would love them anyway. I chose to love as a young girl and as I grew up I continued to choose to love!!! I loved to sing "This Little Light of Mine" so I wanted my light to shine. Mama always said, "If you keep negative things out of your heart, your light will shine. Beauty is what's in your heart!! Keep good thoughts and love others. Keep your heart and mind open to receive love and to give love."

I took bribes from my sister, she loved me anyway. I told on my sister, she loved me anyway. My brother and I messed with her things, she loved us anyway.

She always built me up and never tried to break my spirit. She has always supported me, yet she always expressed her honest opinion.

My Sister Hospitalized

When my sister was about 10 years old, her appendix ruptured, and she was in the hospital for about a month. She was so ill that we almost lost her. Our grandmother would be at the hospital when Mama had to work. Our grandmother was a prayer warrior. She prayed continually for my sister. Our grandmother oozed love. To know my grandmother was to love her!!! My sister has that rare blood type so that was another medical challenge. But God!!! After about a month, she came home from the hospital. I was so happy!!!

My "Sissy Wissy"

We are only six years apart. I have always looked up to her for guidance and her opinion. We are different individuals with different personalities, but we realized that. Whether I act on her advice or not, it is important to me that I get it.

I have always loved my sister and tried to be like her when I was small. But Mama told me that Barbie was Barbie and Leola is Leola. Be yourself. Love you as much as you love Barbie. I was always so excited to be with her that I told everything – I just could not keep it to myself. I still like to spend time with my sister.

During a financial difficult time in my life, my sister always supported me. She would visit almost every year when I lived in Texas, especially when Mama was living. When she left, she would hide savings bonds around my house. She would ask how I was doing financially. If I needed something, she would tell me to look in a "hidden spot" where she had left savings bonds for me.

Today, I tease her all the time and shower her with much love and kisses. I like to call it "loving up a person!" Just showering them with love!!! I call her "My Sissy Wissy" and talk baby talk to her sometimes. I call her and sing to her. I send her gifts just because I love and miss her. I love my Sissy Wissy![15]

---

[5] Two are better than one; because they have a good reward for their labour. For if they fall, the one will lift up his fellow; but woe to him that is alone when he falleth; for he hath not another to help him up. Ecclesiastes 4:9-10

CHAPTER 6

My Brother, Johnnie

My younger brother is two years older than me. We have always been very close. We used to be very competitive!

Mama would make us hug, kiss and say, "I love you" before we went to bed at night. She assumed that we had picked on each other during the day. If we were quiet, she knew we were up to something. She always said, "It is natural to disagree sometimes because you are so close in age but know that you are uniquely different. You are never to put your hands on the other!!! Verbal disagreement is normal between family members, but NO physical disagreement is acceptable. Learn to appreciate your different opinions. Love and respect for each other must be the basis for the most lasting relationship."

We had many disagreements and childish pranks. I am amazed today when I think of how spoiled I was, how I treated my brother and the fact that he still loves me!!! And for that, I am very thankful for my brother's love!!!

Papa, Papa, Johnnie Got My Candy

One day I asked Johnnie for some of his candy. He did not want to give me any. So, I started screaming, "Papa, Papa, Johnnie got my candy!" Papa came in and told Johnnie to give me the candy. Johnnie told Papa that the candy was his. I told Papa that the candy was mine. Papa told Johnnie, "Give the Baby her candy." Not being greedy, I ate half of the candy and gave the rest back to Johnnie. Johnnie was so angry at me that he threw the candy in the garbage.

On another occasion, Johnnie had made me angry about something. I started screaming, "Papa, Papa. Johnnie is hitting me!" Papa ran into the room and saw Johnnie on the other side of the room and me laughing and screaming he was hitting me. Papa looked at me. I felt so ashamed!!! Papa just turned and left the room. After that, I never put Papa in the middle of me and Johnnie. Mama knew I was a performer and now Papa knew it too.

Swimming Collateral

One day, I wanted to go swimming. Mama was at work. I had no money. I asked Johnnie for the money (35¢) to go swimming. He said he would loan it to me, but I had to sign an IOU. I signed the IOU and went swimming. Later, he told me that I owed him the money plus he had added my radio as collateral. Well, that was just wrong!!! So, when he left the house, I searched for the IOU and found it and tore it up. When Mama came home, Johnnie told Mama that I owed him money (more than the original 35¢) and that I had put up collateral, just in case, I did not pay him back. I told Mama I didn't know what he was talking about. He went to get the IOU and it was not there. It was not in his hiding place? Again, I told Mama that I didn't know what he was talking about. Mama knew that we both were guilty of lying and trying to manipulate each other. She gave him his money.

Not Me!

On yet another occasion, Johnnie went on top of the roof of the house to get something. I took the ladder down. He could not jump off the roof because it was too high to jump down, so he had to stay up there. When I saw Mama coming, I went into the house and slipped out the back door. I put the ladder back up and went back into the house. Mama saw Johnnie on top of the roof and asked him why was he up there? He told her that I took the ladder down and he could not get down. Naturally, I didn't know what he was talking about. Not me! I walked around the house with Mama and the ladder was on the house. That night, I really had to hug him tightly, tell him I was sorry, I loved him, and kiss him.

Watched Out for Me

When Johnnie went to school games, he would always watch out for me. I was young and wanted to talk to the boys. Even if I did not see Johnnie, I knew he saw me. He would show up and tell me it was time to go of just show up and let me know he was there.

Johnnie was very protective of me. We argued back and forth over the smallest things. But, he did not want me to get punished and sometimes he took the blame. BUT, he got me back!!! "Do it again and I will get you!" he said.

I Missed My Brother

Johnnie and I had never been apart. When he joined the Army, I was so lost. He would call collect and I would accept. I would cry on the phone. I really missed him so much!!! Mama told me she could not afford for me to accept all the collect phone calls, but I accepted every call. Finally, Mama said, "OK. Only talk 2 minutes and hang up." I know she could not pay the bills, but I missed my brother so much, I had to hear his voice and know that he was alright.

I am so thankful that Mama made us kiss and make up and always say "I love you" at night before we went to bed. I raised my children the same way. I have always been thankful to my brother. I love Johnnie so much and I have always been amazed how we can talk about our childhood and laugh. I love my brother, Johnnie![6]

---

[6] Love one another with brotherly affection. Outdo one another in showing honor. Romans 12:10 ESV

CHAPTER 7

My Big Brother, A. J.

*M*y oldest brother, AJ, is 9 years older than me. He stands 6'3" tall. He is the first grandson and the second grandchild of Nannie and Willie Turner. Our Grandmother, Nannie Turner, died when I was about 3 years old. I remember riding in the ambulance taking her to the hospital. I do remember that she was a lovely lady and a very devout Christian. She truly loved God and never said anything bad about anyone. She was soft spoken and had beautiful hair. I don't remember much more about her. My brother knew her and used to tell me about the things she would tell him.

AJ Reflects on our Grandmother

As my brother grew up, Nannie would talk to him about living a righteous life. These are some of the things, she said that he should always remember:

- Never do wrong. You know the difference between right and wrong; difference between what is legal and what is illegal. You must make that decision and stick with it.
- Never steal. One-time Nannie baked some tea cakes. The teacakes had just been taken out of the oven and were still very hot. My brother decided he wanted some. He did not have a bag, so he put them in his pocket. Nannie came into the kitchen and saw that some were missing. Those tea cakes got hotter and hotter in his pocket. She asked him who took the tea cakes. By this time, they were burning his pocket, so he had to take them out. She said, "Never steal again! Just ask for them. Never steal!!!
- Never play dice. She told him this when she was dying. He was 12 years old.
- Get married! Raise a family!
- Always do right by others.
- Stop fighting other people' battles. You do not help a person by fighting their battles. Every man should standup for what he believes in. Standing up for your beliefs is more important than winning.
- Don't pick berries (Don't make bad decisions). When you walk in the woods (through life), snakes (evil people) can be there and you will not see it (recognize what they are) until it's too late. You can always back out. Go back

the way you came and stay out of those bushes (bad places).

- Nannie loved Coke Cola. Cokes were sometimes hard to get but Papa always got them for her. Papa really loved Nannie.
- Nannie never whipped any child. She would grab your ear and twist it; then talk with you about the choices you made. Papa would whip the boys but never the girls.
- Handle your paycheck. Pay your bills first. Be responsible!!

AJ Reflects on Our Grandfather

Papa taught my brother a lot of things that a boy needed to know during those times and some hold true today:

- Don't touch bootleg. One time, papa drunk some bootleg. He took the shortcut home through the nearby cemetery. He fell into an open grave and went to sleep. When he woke up, he saw only dirt, walls of dirt. When he got out of that grave, he never drunk bootleg again. My grandmother told my brother to never drink bootleg!!!

Don't Call Me

My mother always told us not to steal, cheat, lie, or basically do anything illegal. I remember she told my oldest brother that if he did anything illegal, don't call her to come get him out of jail. She said, "Don't do it!! Choose your friends wisely. Choose friends that think like you. Remember that a true friend will not tell you to do anything wrong." She was confident that he would do the right thing!!! Nannie used to talk with my brother also.

The main point of her conversations with him was "Do Right!" We all knew that Nannie was loving and kind, but she was a no-nonsense person. She was a devout person that walked and lived her talk!!! Thus, she expected the same of us even though we did not live up to her standards, but we tried.

My brother's friend did something wrong and said that he was with him. He lied!!! The police came to the house and got my brother and took him to jail. My grandfather told the police that he was home at that time and could not have done anything. Later, the police found out that he did not do anything wrong and called Mama to come get him. Mama said she was not coming. She told the police to keep him for a while to make him think about the company he keeps. They told her to come pick him up that day. But, she picked him up the next day. He did not like being behind bars.

You Can Count on Us

My brother had a brain tumor and we decided to take him to the Mayo Clinic in Rochester, Minnesota. This began many trips on the road to recovery! He had two visits before his surgery. One weekend we went up for an appointment and they decided to do the surgery. Barbie and I had no extra clothes, so we went shopping. We extended our stay at the apartment – unsure of when he would be able to go home. He had his surgery and it was a success! After his surgery, Barbie stayed there, and I went back to Illinois. I commuted every weekend. He stayed in the hospital a month and Barbie stayed there with him. Finally, he was able to go home – to my home to await his follow-up appointment after the surgery. He had two therapists coming in to assist him. He would do his therapy for them – but not for us!

Then it was time to return to Mayo for his follow-up visit. The doctors were excited about how well the surgery went and he was scheduled to come back in 6 months. He could now go home.

I think he was tired of us trying to tell him what to do. We could not get him to exercise, go out shopping or walking, even though when I had my surgery, he was right there telling me I needed to walk and walking with me. When I bugged him, he would do something to make me get out of the room. One day, I decided to watch TV. I held on to the TV remote control. I was not watching what he wanted to watch. So, he did something to irritate me and I left the room. I told him, "I am not speaking to you anymore today!" He smiled and waved. I knew then that he had gotten me!!! Now, he could watch whatever he wanted to watch!!!

When it was time for AJ to go home, we met our other brother, Johnnie, half way between Chicago and Pine Bluff, to transfer AJ. He was so excited to be going home that He got out of my car and WALKED around the building. We could not get him to walk!!! We had to drop him off at the front door of the restaurant.

He has always been free-hearted. Whenever I was travelling through Pine Bluff, he always asked me "how the hanks were" meaning do I need any money. Now, he always liked the best steaks!!! When we went grocery shopping, he put all the best meat in the cart. Only, by the time we got to the cashier, he was missing. We have always been very competitive. So, one time we were shopping, and I put all kinds of things in the cart. By the time he got to the cashier, I happen to be absent. After he paid, I walked up too late to pay!!! Ha, Ha!!!

Our mother raised us to be there for one another. We always have been!!! We have supported one another and shown love all our lives. We argue but we never lose the "love connection" that our mother gave us so many years ago.

I love my big brother!!! My big brother loves me![7]

---

[7] Look how good and how pleasant it is when brothers live together in unity! Psalm 133:1

CHAPTER 8

Down but Not Out!

hen I moved back to Chicago in 1993, I planned to start teaching typing and word processing. I applied for a license for a home school, acquired computers and classroom equipment, prepared all my class plans and was awaiting an inspection. Then, I got ill. I thought that I was having a heart attack, but later I found out that I had acid reflux and had suffered a gastric attack. It thought I was having a heart attack. I did not have any medical insurance. I had to pay for my doctor visits and all the x-rays and heart tests. I had almost depleted my money and I was feeling low. I am usually very upbeat, and I did not like feeling depressed. So, I decided to write myself a letter of encouragement. The following letter was written:

August 18, 1994

Dear Leola,

Do you feed discouraged? Do not feel sad. You are such a moody person that you will have to find ways to cheer yourself up.

Why not change your habits? Don't go home and get in the bed. Go walking. Go shopping (or should I say browsing). Go visit a friend. Clean or rearrange your room. Cook an experimental dish. JOIN A CHURCH!!!

I realize that Life is not always what you want it to be, but it can be a lot worse. Count your blessings each time you start to feel depressed. Let's go over some of your blessings:

> Good Health, at least no heart attack.

> Children are healthy, no drugs/no jail, working or going to school.

> Minimal bills to pay.

> Loving family.

> Good friends.

> New business that needs lots of work and time.

Now isn't that just wonderful. You have so much to be thankful for. Let's look at the things you are depressed over:

> No money.

Well, money is not everything. Just think, if you had to make a choice of deleting something off your thankful list to get money, which one would you delete? Good health? Your family? Your friends? Surely, not the well-being and happiness of your children? So, you see that everything must stay!!! Then you realize that you have everything that is important.

When you feel depressed or alone, read this letter to remember your blessings.

Don't take life so seriously.

Join a church! Work in that church! Study the Word of God!

You have nothing to be depressed about!

You have the most important things in your life!

YOU ARE ALLRIGHT!!!

May the Good Lord Bless and keep you!!! Continue to pray that the Lord will shine down upon you. Pray for your family and friends. Pray for understanding.

And remember, "no human being" on this earth loves you more than I do. As Kojak used to say, who loves you baby? Leola does!!!

Love,

Leola M. Jones

P.S. Years later, I realized that God had a different path for me. The events in my life, people I came to know, places I went, and the things I learned reassured me of God's presence in my life. I went back to church and most important, I learned that all you need is the Lord. Pray for His blessings. What God has for you is for you. He gives us what we need and supplies some of our wants. You will get them according to his schedule, if the blessing you want is for you![8]

---

[8] The heart of man plans his way, but the Lord establishes his steps. Proverb 16:9

CHAPTER 9

My Introduction to Racism

I was always a very friendly and playful child, or so I was told. I lived in a moderate black neighborhood. The bus stop was two blocks from my house. School was within a one-mile walk. A larger grocery store was about 2 blocks away. Everything was so convenient because we lived a couple of miles from downtown.

About 2 blocks north was a small family-owned grocery store. The owners had two daughters. They were the only white children on my street.

One of the sisters and I had become very friendly. When you are little, who you consider your "best friend" is someone you talk with and play with. We talked about our studies and what we were learning. We talked about what we were wearing to school the next day. It did not matter to us that we went to separate schools.

One day my sister was taking me downtown to shop for shoes. This day, we took the bus downtown. When we got on the bus, my sister, her friend and I sat mid-way to the back of the bus. A block after we got on the bus, my white friend and her twin sister got on the bus. When she saw me, she came and sat down next to me. We were both glad to see each other. She sat next to me and we began talking.

The bus driver was looking at us. He called her come to the front of the bus. He said, "Young lady, you can't sit there." Then my friend's sister told her that they must get off the bus. I asked if I could go with them. My friend's sister said that "she knew that I could not go with them". I did not really understand.

My sister later told me about "colored" and "white" sections on the bus. I then realized why the bus driver was angry.

That evening my friend told me that we could no longer be friends. Her parents had told her that she was too old to play with me any longer. She could not visit me again. We could not play together. She was also told that she was not to talk to me. We did not really understand why we could not be friends anymore. This black and white thing was new to us. We had only known each other as friends. This was my first introduction to racism.

Since that encounter, the world has been black and white to me. To dislike a person only because their skin is black is a sin against God. How could "Christian" man-kind love a God they have never seen and hate their fellow man - standing, sitting, walking, living and talking next to them? I promised myself from that day on that I would never dislike a person because of anything other than the person themselves. The color of a person's skin would not define how I felt about the person.

Yes, I have kept my promise. I love ALL people regardless of ethnicity, religion, sexual orientation, . . .[9]

---

[9] Though I speak with the tongues of men and of angels, but have not *love*, I have become sounding brass or a clanging cymbal. ... And now abide faith, hope, *love*, these three; but *the greatest* of these is *love*. 1 Corinthians 13:3 NKJV

CHAPTER 10

My First Accident

*M*y first accident scared me and made me laugh. It showed me a glimpse of myself that I did not know existed. I never thought about how I would react if I found myself in an emergency.

I had a 1974, burgundy, 2-door, hatchback Gremlin. I felt very proud of my first "new" car. I took the car in for its regular maintenance checkup, washed it once a week, let no one eat in it, and took extra care in parking to minimize getting dents in the parking lot. The car was in excellent condition considering it was 5 years old. I always drove the speed limit and drove defensively, cautiously looking out for the other man since I had always been told that "the best way to drive is defensively."

On the way home from college one cold, wintery evening in November, I decided to drive down 123rd Street. I usually took main streets like Halsted, but tonight I needed to hurry home to watch Star Trek on TV. I enjoyed watching the adventures of Captain Kirk and Mr. Spock. It had been snowing for several days and we had about two inches of snow that had fallen earlier that day. The snow had melted and had turned into ice with new snow on top of the ice.

I was driving west on 123rd Street about 8:00 PM. It was dark, yet the white snow made the night seem less foreboding. The street lights were shining brightly giving off good visibility. I noticed a station wagon heading south on Yale Street. The station wagon carried a female driver, a female passenger in the front seat and about four children all talking, screaming, and jumping up and down in the back seat. No seat belts were used by any of the passengers or the driver. Since I purchased my first car with seatbelts, I always made sure my children were buckled up. I had the right-of-way, and the station wagon had the stop sign. As I approached the stop sign, I could see the station wagon approaching 123rd Street. I continued but I slowed my speed, never thinking that the station wagon would not stop at the stop sign.

As my car entered the intersection, travelling about 20 mph, the station wagon arrived at the stop sign. The station wagon did not stop at the stop sign. It continued into the intersection and struck my car on the passenger side, mid-way the door. The impact knocked my car out of control. My car spun around and by the time I regained control of the car, it was facing east on 123rd Street. The station wagon had spun around, slightly in a ditch, also was headed east. I could hear the children screaming and crying, "Mama, Mama." The distance between my car and the station wagon ranged about 2-3 car lengths. The motor of both our cars continued to run.

Concerned for the children, I immediately jumped out of my car and ran toward the station wagon. As I approached the station wagon, the driver turned the wheel of the wagon to get out of the ditch and drove off. I stood in the street, dazed for a few seconds, watching her driving off. It seemed as if I had stood there a long, long time, however, only a few seconds had passed. Suddenly, without thinking, I ran to my car and took off to catch up with the wagon.

She went down 2 blocks, turned left, and then turned right. Following close behind her, I caught a glimpse of her license plate, ..." We were speeding over 30 mph, driving recklessly. When I turned the last corner, I almost lost control of my car. I assumed she turned down another street when she noticed no lights were behind her. I gave up the chase.

I drove home feeling anger at the woman for hitting my car and driving off; stunned that I would pull a reckless "Starsky and Hutch" chase up and down the streets; and concerned over the possible harm we could have caused people and property. When I got home, I looked at the damage to my car. My "pride and joy" could be fixed in a day or so, but the damage to my pride needed time to heal.

I went into the house and gave my family the details of the "encounter" and we all laughed. The next day, I went to the police station to report the accident. I gave the police the license number of the car and called my insurance company to report the accident. Naturally, I omitted the "Starsky and Hutch" chase. The damage to my car (a dent in the passenger door) was minimal, but my pride was hurt much more.

I often wondered about the woman driver. I feel sorry for her children. What a careless mother she must be! I wondered how a person could leave an accident? How could a mother risk danger to her children? How could I have chased that car? We never know what we will do when we find ourselves in unusual circumstances. If this happens again, would I chase the car again? Would you? I now know that you can get another car, but LIFE cannot be replaced.[10]

---

[10] Trouble pursues the sinner, but the righteous are rewarded with good things. Proverbs 13:21 NIV

CHAPTER 11

Accidents Along the Way

Fell in Ravine

To walk to school, we could walk about 8-10 blocks or cross the ravine. To cross the ravine, you had to "walk the pipe" because there was no bridge. Now, we were told not to go that way because it could be dangerous. I could not swim. Running late for school one day, I decided to go that way. It had been raining and the water was higher than usual. The bigger boys would take the smaller children across. With the water being so high, I was scared. I was the last one to cross.

All the others had made it across fine! But, not me! I fell in! My cousin, my brother and his friend helped the other children. My brother was shocked when I fell in. His friend and my cousin jumped in the water and pulled me out. I was so scared!!! I also knew that I was in trouble because I was told not to go this way. I had to go back home and change my clothes. Mama was at work, so I changed and went to school . . . the regular way. That incident prompted me to learn to swim. However, it took two years to just learn to float because I was a little afraid of putting my head being under the water.

Again, Mama knows best!!!

Fell of the Roof

Why I went on top of the house, I just don't know. More than likely, Johnnie and I was up to something! I do know that I fell off the roof and knocked a hole in my head. You could see the hole in my head! I did not go to the hospital. Someone told Papa to put some ashes into the hole. Later, when Mama came home, she took me to the doctor. The doctor said it looked alright and that was it. Now, I have an excuse!! If I acted strange after that incident, I could blame it on having a hole in my head.[11]

---

[11] The way of a fool [is] right in his own eyes: but he that hearkeneth unto counsel [is] wise. Proverbs 12:15 KJV

CHAPTER 12

Faith

aith means a lot of things to different people. Many people use the term faith, but few of us know exactly what it means. Most of us never stop to think exactly how important this word is to our daily lives. To get a closer insight into what it means, we need to define it according to the dictionary; we need to recognize it in our daily lives; and we need to learn to put our trust in it. First, what does the word faith mean?

Webster's Seventh New Collegiate Dictionary (1965) defines faith as "firm belief in something for which there is no proof; something is believed, especially with strong conviction; especially in a system of religious beliefs." The synonym for faith given is "belief." To say you have "blind trust" when you believe in the **Word of God** and know that all things work together according to the scripture. Webster's definition is good, but how does this definition relate to me?

Many times, I have heard the old saying "Keep the Faith." I always answered that I would, but what was I "keeping"? This slang term means to "hang in there" or "hold fast for a change is going to come". Faith begins within and illuminates outward. It strengthens our every action and thought. Faith is believing in God, yourself, others and trusting that everything will work out for the best in the end. A good example of "keeping the faith" is when others are promoted, and your chance never comes. You believe that one day success will find you and until it's your turn to succeed, you "should keep the faith" and that is when your trust in God and the Holy Spirit will lead you. What would life be like without faith?

If you have ever been without faith, you must have been a very lonely person. Faith brings light into darkness, hope to the hopeless, and it warms the lonely souls and wraps a protective arm around us. When we have done all we can do, and we can't go any further, faith removes the barriers and let us pass. Sometimes if the barrier is not moved, faith allows us to go through it without hardship. Worry is a human weakness and even though we have confidence, we believe/trust, and have strong convictions, we worry about the outcome. We worry in vain because if we believe it will happen, it will happen. We just do not know when it will happen. When you need to feed your children and you have no money, faith sends an unexpected check or gift to your home. When you are sick and can't get well, faith makes you feel better. Look at what faith did for Job!

Faith, whether defined by Webster, slang, or experience, is many things to many people. Faith is believing in something regardless of whether you can get it or not. Faith is "blind trust." Faith is love. Faith is confidence. Faith is letting your light shine by believing good over bad; faith allows you to hold onto your convictions and not waiver from your chosen beliefs; doing what you know is right; and faith is putting your "heart and soul" into your convictions and standing up for what you believe is right. Faith is loyalty, allegiance, sureness, acceptance, truth, and much more. Isn't faith wonderful!

(This was written in 1977. This was a very stressful time in my life. Without "Faith" I do not know how I would have made it that year. God sent me Angels when my car broke down; placed me at a good job; gave me a loving family and friends who supported me.)[12]

---

[12] When you go through deep waters, I will be with you. Isaiah 43:2

CHAPTER 13

My Special Place

*M*y bedroom is very special to me. It is my haven, my office, my special room. Your home is supposed to be your castle, but your home represents your entire household. Your bedroom reflects you alone.

My bedroom is made up of a queen-sized bed, chest, dresser, night stand, clothes bin and stool. My window has white mini-blinds and hunter and light green shear curtains to allow sunlight to enter the room. Matching comforter is dark green and light green. My bedroom set was purchased in 1969. It held up very well and still looked good except for a few nicks received from moving several times. Not being a material person, I have enjoyed my bedroom for many years. When I decided to move back to Houston in 2012, I decided to purchase a new bedroom set. Both sets are dark brown/Mahoney colors.

My bedroom looks like I feel at times. Sometimes, it is neat and clean when I am in a good mood (usually), and when I feel overwhelmed, it is cluttered and disorderly.

Before I retired, I would arrive home from a busy, demanding and stressful day. Sometimes I would go to my room and rest for 30 minutes. Other times, I would stop in the kitchen; cook or heat me some dinner. I would sit and relax in the kitchen for about an hour or more. I did not plan my evenings. I ate what was prepared or I cooked. Sometimes, I would purchase my dinner on the way home. Once home, I really did not want to go outside again. If I had to go outside, I would park in front of the house and not in the garage.

After all my chores are completed, the evening is all mine. I usually lie in bed, read my magazines or since I was almost a career-student, I would do my homework, or I would just watch television (or let the television watch me).

I can stay in my bedroom for days only going out to get food and drink. At night, when I cannot sleep, I lay awake and think. I feel safe in my room. I feel loved in my room. I can look around the wall and see my life; my children at different ages, myself when I was younger, my mother, grandfather, my siblings and other relatives.

I like my bedroom because it is me. I feel more relaxed and comfortable in this room than any other room in the house. When I feel depressed, lonely, or sometimes when I just need time to think, I go to my room. I can lie in bed and think. I plan, anticipate, dream, wish, hope, ponder, and I pray. Everyone prays for something. I pray for my children, my family and friends, and myself. I read the Bible to seek a Word from the Lord. I feel good!

The most important reason why my bedroom is special to me is - IT IS ME. All I have been, and all that I hope to be, is reflected in my bedroom.

Bible verses are all over the room. When I look at one, I remember what was happening and why that verse means so much to me. I never want to forget how far the Lord has brought me. My favorite verse is "24 This is the day which the LORD hath made; we will rejoice and be glad in it." Psalm 118:24. This is the day that the Lord has made – and I will rejoice and be glad in it! I remember that God healed my breast cancer! When I look back, I see that God has never left me alone![13]

---

[13] The angel of the LORD encamps around those who fear him and delivers them. Psalms 34:7 NKJV

CHAPTER 14

Drop Dead

*T*here are some people that you meet in your lifetime that really impacts your life. People can be so kind, loving, compassionate and humble.

I met her at my job in 1997. She was from Belize. She was so loving, compassionate and caring with a strong personality. We became almost instant friends.

She was so devoted to her only daughter. When her daughter married, she gained a son. After a few years, she was so excited to become a grandmother of a beautiful baby boy. Her devotion was shared with her grandson. She was so proud of her grandson and wanted to experience all that she could of his life.

Soon, she retired and committed herself to making sure that her grandson did not have any negative day-care experiences, so she was always there for him. She had so much love in her heart that whenever she talked of her grandson, you could feel the emotion and hear the excitement and love in her voice.

I have so many good memories of working with her. Now, she could be very emotional, expressive, frank and honest, about how she felt about you or something that you had done. Many days, I would hear her voice as she was "blessing" someone about something.

Often, we would bring "pot luck" lunches and eat together. I was always impressed with her knowledge of cooking. She believed in cleanliness. Her house was always spotless and orderly.

She had a big giving heart!!! She expressed so much love for her church and the Father there. When he died, she said how much she would miss him. I think that she loved caring for people and tried to help those she met and became concerned about. I am thankful she chose me as a friend. She was very generous with my grandson at Christmas. After a visit to her home one year around Christmas, he began to ask about the "nice lady" he had met. From that point, he always asked about the "nice lady."

When I think of what my friend told me one day, I am filled with laughter. Once she was upset that someone questioned her honesty and integrity. I could never understand why anyone would question her integrity. Just knowing her for a short time, I knew she was very honest and would never do anything against any human being. Well, she told this person to "Hurry up and follow the father." The father was dead. I have never heard the expression "drop dead" sound so polite than I did when she repeated the conversation to me. She loved this person very much!!! She just had a way of expressing herself!!!

When I was informed that she had died, I could only smile. She was so full of life, love, compassion, honesty, and truly she loved God! She loved her church! She loved her friends and neighbors! And, how very much she loved her family!!!

Many people will come into our lives, but very few will leave a lasting impact on our lives and our ideas. I believe that God wants us to love each other as he loves us (John 13:34) and that we should always treat others the way we want to be treated (Luke 6:31). She embellished all this to me! I am blessed to have had her in my life as a wonderful and loving friend.[14]

---

[14] Do nothing out of selfish ambition or vain conceit. Rather, in humility value others above yourselves. Philippians 2:3 NIV

CHAPTER 15

Marriage Should Add, Not Subtract

My husband was my friend. I could talk to him about almost anything. Looking back, I realized that I was so naïve and innocent that I was in love with a dream. I always dreamed that I would grow up, finish college preferably becoming a teacher, marry the man of my dreams, have two children (boy and girl), and live happily ever after. As you can see I have always been a dreamer!!!

Well, I got married before I finished college. I got an administrative job. I knew from taking shorthand and typing in high school that I liked administrative tasks. I had two children – a daughter and 6 years later a son. I liked married life. But, nothing stays the same. I grew up! I remembered my dream and wanted to fulfill all of it! I had to go back to college! My husband did not want me to go. I suggested to him that he could go to college and later I would go back to college. But, he had a good job and did not want to go to college. I always wanted to get a college degree.

So, I decided to go back to college. It would take me many years to finish, but I kept going. I changed my major several times. Each time I transferred to a different department, I would change my studies so that I could be an asset to that department. I always wanted to do my best in whatever I was doing. Papa used to say, "If you are a ditch digger, be the best ditch digger you can be. If you do your best in whatever you do, you can be proud of your work." I always remembered that.

My husband used to buy my clothes. He had better taste than I did on somethings. He took good care of his family. He worked hard to support the family. He took the children on outing, air shows, the zoo, and others. He loved us!!!

I know now that when you are young, you say half of what you truly think and half of what you think will not offend the other person. My husband worked nights, so I would sometimes go by my father-in-law's house. I became very close to him and the youngest son, Louis, who was still at home. Louis has always been so special to me. When I was pregnant, he would walk over to our apartment because I wanted a soda pop. I will always love him for all his love and kindness.

I had the most stressful time of my life. My son had undergone open heart surgery. My mother had an aneurysm in the brain which left her unable to walk. My husband's mother died when he was very young. He did not realize how close I was to my mother. I was living day-by-day. I needed support!!! I was overloaded!!! At this point, what I needed, I could not give to others. I could not get it from my husband!

My husband and I thought we would grow old together. He said we would be sitting on our porch in a rocking chair watching our grandchildren play. But, that would not happen for us.

I am thankful for my husband. I am thankful for our children. I was happy when my husband remarried and wished him well. I never remarried. I have led a full life and thank God, I am still living and enjoying LIFE![15]

---

[15] And be kind to one another, tenderhearted, forgiving one another, even as God in Christ forgave you. Ephesians 4:32 KJV

CHAPTER 16

My Cousins

My mother had two sisters and a brother. As it would be, our ages correlated to some of the siblings' children age groups, with some gaps.

Growing Up

I was very close to my cousins. The cousins in my age group included 1 boy (Charles) and 2 girls (Freddie Mae and me). I loved to spend the night at my Aunt Lena's house. She had 6 girls and 2 boys. The house was full of laughter and noise. At night, we could talk and laugh until we went to sleep. The bed was crowed – full of love and companionship.

Freddie and I would walk backward and forth between our homes. I would walk her half-way home and she would walk me half-way home. We both loved to talk so we walked and talked about our dreams and hopes for our future.

Our Cornbread Disagreement

We got along fine! But, came that terrible day when we had the biggest disagreement of our young lives. We were about 13 or 14 years old. Freddie was at my house. We were both hungry and I found some greens or beans (can't remember which) and one tiny piece of cornbread. Well, Freddie thought that since she was my guest, I should give her the tiny piece of cornbread. I thought that I really wanted that cornbread and it was just TOO small to share. So, I didn't give it to her. That was our first and only argument in our lives. Over the years, we laugh at how serious and angry we were about the 'tiny piece" of cornbread, that I said was too small to share. We never thought that neither one of us should have eaten it since it was not enough for the two of us. It should not have been that important, but it was!

What lesson did we learn from that disagreement? I had several options: 1) give her the cornbread since she was my guest/cousin/friend; 2) selfishly eat the cornbread; 3) share the tiny piece of cornbread, or 4) neither one of us should eat the cornbread.

Years later, we still laugh about that "tiny piece" of cornbread. Regardless of how many years that we do not see each other or even talk with each other, as soon as we reconnect with each other, it is just like when we are young again. I love my cousin and my cousin loves me. That will never change!!!

Reconnect with Your Family

Just recently, we started conversing over the phone and it was "just like yesterday" and the closeness we had as children is still there. She came to visit at my home and I planned to visit her soon. We both like to talk so we have a grand time conversing with each other. I am thankful that the love connection that was developed so many years ago between me and my cousin, and her other siblings, will last us a lifetime. We talk on the phone for hours. We have grown even closer as adults.

I remember the last conversation I had with Freddie's sister Jeanette. I admired a pair of earrings she was wearing. She took them off and gave them to me. I still have them. Jeanette died shortly after that. With us growing up and leaving home, I did not know a lot of addresses. When I got to Pine Bluff, I used to visit my cousin Earsalene and my Aunt Dora. I think what we miss the most is not visiting and communicating with each other often enough. Reconnect with your family or friends. Thank God for Love![16]

---

[16] How good and pleasant it is when God's people live together in unity. Psalm 133:1 NIV

CHAPTER 17

A Friend

*J*n the summer of 1962, I went swimming at Townsend Park. I met a boy whom I was instantly attracted to. There was another boy that I had been talking to but after I met him, I only had eyes for him. He walked me home and that was the beginning of a great friendship that has lasted over 55 years.

When he went to Vietnam, I missed him very much. I sent pre-sweetened Kool Aid and magazines to him. He sent me a Japanese kimono and a charm, which I still have today. He was wounded just before his tour was over.

Time passed on and we did not keep in touch. He moved to Michigan and I moved to Illinois.

After he returned from the Army, I saw him a few times. I felt that he was not as interested in me as I was in him. During that time, I met my future husband who I had also known in Arkansas. He moved from the country and lived close to one of my aunts. He later moved to Illinois and lived across the street from my sister.

By this time, my friend had gotten a job and began his new life in Michigan. Over the years, we would lose touch with each other but would reconnect. I married and had children. He married and had children.

Years later, I had divorced my husband and reconnected with him, mostly phone conversations. I think the longest time we did not talk or see each other was about 10 years.

Over the years, I have been able to talk to him about almost anything, my desires, life problems, illnesses, children, career plans, and most important, about how God was working in our lives.

Now many years later, our children are grown. He is a widower. I am a divorcee. I still look upon him as someone I always want in my life. His friendship has always been very important to me.

Through the years, we have enlisted advice and comments from each other on major problems in our life. He has given me good advice over the years and I hope that he can say the same for me.

What do I think of him after all these years? I realize that people are put into our lives sometimes for a season and others are put there throughout our life time. I think we both have blessed each other by listening, caring, advising and supporting each other through all the years.

If you have a friendship that lasts over 55 years, you are truly blessed!!! We are here to love others. To support them, to be honest with them, and never to judge them. God places people in your life for a reason. I think that God placed him in my life because he has strengthened me many times when I was down by supporting me; telling me that things will work out and just to continue to trust God!!! As a matter of fact, when I was not in church, through discussions with him, I went back to church. His friendship has meant a lot to me. He hears me when I talk. I think that we all need a friend that is impartial but honest when we need honesty. Thank God for a friend![17]

---

[17] Love one another with brotherly affection. Outdo one another in showing honor. Roman 12:10 ESV

CHAPTER 18

People Placed in My Life

$\mathcal{I}$ have often expressed the fact that God has blessed me with so many beautiful people in my life. I thank God for that every day.

I have always loved people. I always loved to talk. So, where ever I go, whether alone or with others, I am usually very comfortable. I will find someone to talk with.

I have so many friends. Once you are my friend, you are a friend for life. I may not always send a note, card, text, email or call my friend, but I will always love them. I realize that we all have busy lives. The occasional contact lets us know that we are still in the land of the living and doing well.

My wonderful friends, Alice, who died in 2012; Beverly who died in 2015; and Loret who died in 2014. My first Chicago friend,

Dorothy. My first friend when I worked at Illinois Bell, Shirley. My friends from BP: Deborah, Linda, Cathy, Marguerite. My special friends from St. Mark Church in Illinois: Betty, Silver, Mary, Mrs. Tucker, Lovie, Dolores, Minister Hatch, Roberta, Annie, and many more. From the time I lived in Houston the first time: Lisa, Than Nhi, Coleen, Dora, Diane, Marilyn, Willie Mae, Gloria and many more. The wonderful members of Seniors on the Move. From my current church, Dorothy, Sarah, Ida, Leonora, Nedra, Sis. McClain, Martha, and my cancer survivor's group, along with Good Hope's wonderful staff of ministers and many more.

My wonderful friends at the Center: Cherry, Sandy, Barbara, Joyce, Mira, Marcy, Laura, Marie, Lucie, Deidre, Ashley, and many, many more.

I wanted to put everyone's names down, but there were too many for the page. My point – I have been truly blessed with many wonderful friends!! I have been blessed with so many beautiful people in my life.

Thank you for Loving Me!

CHAPTER 19

My Angels

We grew up in church. As a child, we had no option: Go to church on Sunday!!! Sunday School and BTU!!! No church on Sunday, no recreational activities during the week.

We know that we do not deserve salvation because we are good, but because Jesus gave his life for us, while we were still sinners. We have received salvation through the Blood of Jesus Christ.

We see-saw through live. We try to be good; we slip and become embarrassed; we restart our engines and slip again. Once I joined this church in Chicago and I was going regularly and joined different ministries. I slipped!!! I was so disappointed that I said/did something that I thought I would never do again. I was so hurt! We try to be good and treat people the right way we want to be treated, but we will never achieve 100% in this lifetime. One of the ladies from the church called me and told me to come back to church. She said, "Whatever you think you did, God knows all. He knows your heart. Come back to church. God wants you." I called her "My Granny Angel." I went back and tried to be the best I could, while realizing that, if I keep my heart open, my mind on the Word of God, my steps walking in the light, when I slip, I will get back up and try until I get it right. So, each slip should make us stronger."

My sister always went to the doctor's office with me. My sister waited for me in the waiting room while I visited with the doctor. The doctor told me I had breast cancer. He gave me some literature to read and said we would talk about my options at the next meeting. After I came out of the doctor's office, I waved for my sister to follow me and we walked to the elevator. A lady was standing at the elevator and she started talking about how the Lord had healed her breast cancer. She praised the Lord in the elevator, walked to my car, and stood awhile at my car praising the Lord!!! After a few minutes, she hugged me and left.

When she left, my sister asked me who was she. I said, "She is my Angel!!! The doctor just told me that I have breast cancer and His Angel has just reminded me that God is a Healing God." We stood at the car for a while but never saw her drive out of the parking lot. We then got in my car and left. What an experience! *The doctor had just told me that I had breast cancer and my Angel had just told me that God heals!!! Wow!!!*

What a blessing! We can drown ourselves in pity and "why me?" or we can live everyday believing "God has the last say in our lives. We control very little in our life, BUT God has complete control over what he allows to happen to us. He loves us in-spite of our lack of commitment to His Word. He knows we try.

I am a talker. When I told my family and friends that I had breast cancer, I told them that it was not going to be fatal. My Angel reminded me that God Heals!!! Then I added, "Nevertheless, not my will but God's will be done." (Luke 22:42)

God brought me through that and I can look back and realize that he was with me through many trials and tribulations. He has never left me alone!!! I thank Him for my Angel!

After my surgery and recuperation, I returned to work. I was so tired and needed help during my recuperation period. My sister was contracted to work with me. My sister would pick me up and would drive to the Metra train for us to take to downtown Chicago. After work, she would drop me off. I would just sit in the car talking. Later, I told my sister that I was so tired that I just did not have the energy to get out of the car. I would go in the house, heat my prepared frozen meal, eat and sit until time to go to bed.

During this time, I decided to enroll in Roosevelt University's Paralegal Program. I would leave work and go to class. Usually I got home about 10 PM or if I missed my train, 11 PM. I was still tired. The walk to class and back to the train station was draining what little energy I had. I met other students there that was taking the train and some of them would carry my books for me. I would try to do a little homework on the train so that I would not go to sleep on the train. I would get off the train and drive the 7-8 blocks home. I would park in the garage and go in the back door. I always noticed that my neighbor's den light was on most nights when I got in. Later I found out that he knew what days I went to school and was looking out for me. I graduated with honors. I earned A's in all but one class where I earned a B.

Years later, I realized that my Angel never left me. I explained to my sister how tired I had been. I just did not have the energy to get out of her car. She said she wondered why I sat in her car talking so long. But, being my sister, she did not rush me to get out of her car. We have always supported each other, and she must have sensed something was wrong. I could not have made it without my Angel!!!

Then I remembered when my mother died. I thought something was wrong with me because I did not grief for Mama. I truly loved my mother very much. Then I realized that my Angel took me past it. For months after Mama died, I would get up and sit in her recliner. Then I would get ready and go to work. I used to get up at the same time to bathe her, get her out of bed and give her something to eat and drink before I left for work. My Angel took me past grieving! I did everything I could for my mother. I loved her so much. Just thinking of her makes me feel good. In my heart and mind, I will always think of Mama as a wonderful, loving, and giving mother. That's why Love is so great! Love never dies! It ignites a warmth in your heart that you can take where ever you go for the rest of your life. I am so proud of my children. I know they love me, and I tell them every day that I love them. The memories I want them to remember are not about material things but about relationship building with others:

Loving kindness, thoughtfulness, consistency, availability, dependability, and other things that will help us grow into loving human beings. Thank God for a wonderful, loving and kind mother!! Thank God for my Angels![18]

---

[18] *This is the day* which the LORD *hath made*; we will rejoice and be glad in it. Psalms 119:24

CHAPTER 20

I Am So Thankful

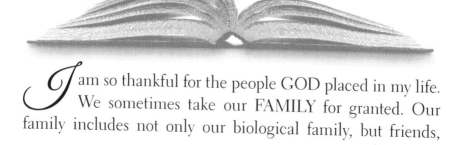

I am so thankful for the people GOD placed in my life. We sometimes take our FAMILY for granted. Our family includes not only our biological family, but friends, neighbors, coworkers, church members, even the strangers that we meet whom we choose to love.

We must choose to love!!! As Papa used to tell us, "Do unto others as you wish them to do unto you. If you can just follow this simple rule, you will have a great life." You will get more out of life. Plant love. Plant compassion. Plant forgiveness. Plant understanding. Plant positive thoughts and not negative thoughts.

Remember DB UG – Down with the Bad, Up with the Good! It is a "work-in-progress life-style" we must all adopt. Practice makes perfect! When we slip, we get back up and start again. That's what makes life worth living. We learn from our successes and failures.

I chose LOVE!!! I had no choice – I always want to LOVE!!! I refuse to hate! Make your choice and you will find it is a beautiful life!

Thank God for Love!!! Thank God for Mama, Papa and my entire family!

Thank God for all the wonderful people in my life!

I find something every day to laugh about![19]

---

[19] A good [man] leaveth an inheritance to his children's children: and the wealth of the sinner [is] laid up for the just. Proverbs 13:22 KJV

Printed in the United States
By Bookmasters